Short Stack Editions | Volume 26

Peanuts

by Steven Satterfield

Short Stack Editions

Publisher: Nick Fauchald
Creative Director: Rotem Raffe
Editor: Kaitlyn Goalen
Copy Editor: Abby Tannenbaum
Wholesale Manager: Erin Fritch

ISBN 978-0-9975321-6-6

Printed in Virginia
February 2017

Table of Contents

Sweets

When it comes to proselytizing ingredient-focused cooking, Steven Satterfield is uniquely suited to the task. At his restaurant, Miller Union, in Atlanta, the hallmark characteristic of the menu is a dedication to its source material. Each plate tells the story of its main components, with as little interference as possible.

All of that is to say that there are dozens of different Short Stack Editions that Steven could have written with brilliant reverence—such is his appreciation and understanding of this approach to cooking. So we were particularly excited when he narrowed down his pick to peanuts, an ingredient that hides in plain sight.

To many, the peanut operates more as a snack or a condiment in the kitchen rather than as the centerpiece of a meal. But the reason for Steven's attraction to the legume becomes apparent through recipes like Peanut Pasta with Broccoli & Peanut Breadcrumbs and Roasted Delicata Squash with Peanut-Sesame-Squash-Seed Dukkah—which demonstrates that this nutrient-dense ingredient is as versatile and self-contained as our most relied-upon staples, such as eggs or rice. It can form the basis of an entire meal thanks to its unique biological makeup.

In Steven's hands, the peanut is more than just a convenient source of protein or a school lunch tradition. His recipes show us the true merit of an ingredient-based approach: turning humble ingredients into exciting discoveries.

—The Editors

Introduction

If you ever find yourself driving down a rural road in the Southern United States during the middle of summer, you'll most likely see a "Hot Boiled Peanuts" sign along the way. I suggest you pull over and grab a bag so you can experience one of the South's favorite rituals.

It's also the experience that cemented my love of peanuts. When I was growing up in Georgia, my family made an annual pilgrimage to the beach, and we'd always stop at roadside produce stands for peaches, tomatoes, sweet corn—and always for boiled peanuts. Those sweet, briny, creamy kernels were so addictive, and inevitably, I would end up with boiled peanut juices on my shirt and there'd be a scattering of peanut shells on the floorboards of the car. But it was 100 percent worth the mess, and made the drive more adventurous.

I was surprised to discover that most folks outside the South are unfamiliar with this version of peanuts. Instead, peanut butter is the more common entry point. I have no shortage of my own childhood peanut butter memories; in fact, I still crave the peanut butter and marshmallow toast, broiled until golden and puffed, that my mother made us as a Saturday snack.

It wasn't until later in life, when I began cooking professionally, that I realized these two childhood delights, boiled peanuts and peanut butter, perfectly sum up what I love about focusing on peanuts as the main ingredient: They are unbelievably versatile, even with the simplest preparation. They have an unmistakable taste, and can bring that distinctive flavor, texture, crunch, sweetness, saltiness or nuttiness to a dish, depending on how you use them.

And even though both boiled peanuts and peanut butter feel just about as American as apple pie, peanuts actually originated in South America, with the oldest evidence of peanuts tracing back to Peru. Peanuts are now widely grown in China, India, Africa, the Americas and the South Pacific. This global cultivation means that peanuts play a starring role in dozens of food cultures, so there's no shortage of inspiration when it comes to cooking them in new ways. In the United States, peanuts are grown in the South, with the largest production in Georgia, which happens to be my home state.

What excites me about cooking with peanuts is their adaptability in a recipe. For the recipes in this book, I looked to the local traditions I grew up with, but I also borrowed from international food cultures. Exploring peanuts from so many angles only solidified my love for them even more: These legumes go with bold flavors such as chiles, ginger, garlic, fruits, spices and chocolate, but also add subtle nutty tones and a welcome crunch to vegetables, side dishes and snacks. They are a source of protein, a nut butter, a snack, a flour, an oil, a ground cover, a soil enricher and a flavor enhancer of many recipes.

I hope this book lends you as much inspiration as peanuts have lent me.

—*Steven Satterfield*

Recipes

Peanut Varieties

Runner

The most widely grown peanut in the United States, with medium-size kernels, a sweet taste and excellent roasting qualities. It is the base of most peanut butter production and the most common peanut grown in Georgia, South Carolina, Alabama and Florida.

Valencia

The least common peanut in the United States, with bright red skin and three to four kernels per shell. Valencia accounts for less than one percent of peanut production and is mostly grown in New Mexico and Texas.

Spanish

A very small redskin variety, often used in candies or snacks or as peanut butter. It has a high oil content and is predominantly grown in Texas and Oklahoma.

Virginia

With the largest kernels of all the peanuts, these are also categorized as cocktail nuts and are mostly grown in the Carolinas and Virginia.

In the Shell

Green peanuts

Freshly dug peanuts with a high moisture content. Very perishable and must be refrigerated and used within 7 to 10 days.

Dried peanuts

Green peanuts that have been dried in the shell to reduce humidity and extend shelf life.

Out of the Shell

Raw peanuts

Dehydrated peanuts in the shell or shelled with skin-on kernels.

Raw blanched peanuts

Dehydrated shelled peanuts with the skins removed.

Dry-roasted peanuts

Dehydrated and roasted peanut kernels with no oil.

Oil-roasted peanuts

Peanuts roasted with vegetable or peanut oil for a crispier product with a higher fat content.

Other Peanut Products

Peanut butter

Peanut puree, with or without the skins. Peanut butter can be made with raw or roasted peanuts, and oil is usually added for a less dry texture. Peanut butter is most commonly sold in two styles, creamy or crunchy, and sometimes salt and/or sugar is added. The recipes in this book call for natural peanut butter with no sugar added.

Peanut oil

Peanut fat that is separated and clarified for cooking.

Peanut flour

Defatted peanut meal, often a by-product of making peanut oil.

Boiled Peanuts

Freshly dug "green" peanuts are what most folks use for boiling since they carry a higher moisture content and tenderize more quickly than dried peanuts, which are available later in the season. I love a plain boiled peanut, but the vinegar in this recipe balances all the salt and adds a nice subtle tang that makes it impossible to eat just one. There's also the joy of watching someone try his or her first boiled peanut. Once, I showed up to a party in New York City with a bag of boiled peanuts. While this gift would be perfectly normal in my hometown of Atlanta, the Manhattanites looked at them with intrigue. As I watched a young woman wince when she popped a few peanuts in her mouth and crunched down on them, shells and all, I quickly realized I was in a room full of boiled-peanut virgins. And so began my lifelong role of professional peanut-eating tutor. It's just one of many peanut tricks I hope to impart in the span of these pages. Here's your first lesson: To eat boiled peanuts, crack open the shell with two fingers (or your teeth), suck out any liquid inside, then pop the peanuts in your mouth, discarding the shells.

2½ pounds green peanuts in the shell, picked over for dirt and debris

1½ cups kosher salt

1 cup apple cider vinegar

In a large stockpot set over high heat, combine the peanuts, salt, vinegar and 6 quarts of water and bring to a boil. Reduce the heat to maintain a simmer. Cover and cook for 4 to 5 hours, or until the peanuts are tender. They should not have any crispness or texture left to them, but should be completely creamy. Serve hot, cold or at room temperature. Refrigerate until ready to eat, either in the cooking liquid or drained, for up to 1 week.

Note: If you cannot find green peanuts near you, order them from our friends at Hardy Farms (hardyfarmspeanuts.com) or the Lee Brothers (boiledpeanuts.com). You can also take the busy professional's approach and order delicious already-boiled peanuts from those sources and have them shipped to your front door. I won't judge.

Dry-Roasted Peanuts

Dry-roasted or oil-roasted peanuts are available in just about every supermarket, health food store and highway gas station. But if you turn the packaging around and read the back label, you might see ingredients such as onion powder, garlic powder, yeast, maltodextrin, sugar or corn syrup muddying up the flavor. The recipes in this book are best with additive-free roasted peanuts, so here's a recipe to roast peanuts yourself if you can't find them in the store.

---

3 cups raw shelled peanuts, either blanched or with the skin on

Preheat the oven to 300° and place a rack in the center position. Spread the raw peanuts in a single layer on a rimmed baking sheet. Roast for 15 to 20 minutes, rotating the baking sheet once halfway through the cooking time, until the peanuts are lightly browned and fragrant. Store the peanuts in an airtight container in a cool, dry place for up to 3 weeks.

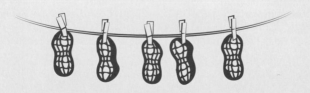

Homemade Peanut Butter

My first attempt at making peanut butter was a disaster. I started in the food processor, then transferred everything to the blender and ended up with dry, sticky peanut butter and too many dirty dishes. Honestly, it was a pain in the ass, and I decided that no one would ever make it. When I described my frustration to my recipe tester, Tamie Cook, she just smiled and said she had a really easy peanut butter recipe that I'd love. If you prefer DIY peanut butter over store-bought, this one is for you. Thanks, Tamie. (A note: You can use this peanut butter in any of the recipes in this book that call for creamy peanut butter.)

2 cups shelled dry-roasted peanuts (page 13; works best using warm, just-roasted peanuts)

1 tablespoon honey

1 teaspoon fine sea salt

2 tablespoons peanut oil

makes 1½ cups

In the bowl of a food processor, process the peanuts for 1 minute. Turn the motor off and scrape the side of the bowl with a rubber spatula. Process for another minute, then stop and scrape the side of the bowl again. Add the honey and salt and process 1 minute longer, then stop and scrape the side of the bowl again. With the motor running, slowly drizzle in the oil. Stop and scrape down the side of the bowl once more. Continue to process and scrape one or two more times, until a smooth paste forms. Refrigerate in an airtight container for up to 3 weeks.

Peanut & Whole Grain Bowl

I think of this as a catchall dish for random whole grains in your pantry combined with a few sliced raw vegetables, greens and, of course, the mighty peanut. I like to use any combination of millet, farro, bulgur, quinoa or sorghum grain. The boiled peanuts add umami, depth and creaminess while boosting nutrients and protein in this already healthy vegetarian bowl.

2 cups cooked whole grains (about 1 to 1½ cups dry)

1 cup shelled boiled peanuts (page 12), measured after shucking

¼ cup thinly sliced radishes

¼ cup thinly sliced carrots

1 cup roughly chopped arugula, turnip tops, radish tops or carrot tops (or a mix)

2 teaspoons fresh lemon juice

2 tablespoons extra-virgin olive oil

Flaky sea salt and freshly ground black pepper

Herbs of your choice, such as basil, tarragon and/or parsley

serves 2

Cook the grains following basic water-to-grain ratios or cooking directions on the package. If you're using more than one type of grain, cook each type separately to control texture, and add a little salt to the cooking water to season the grains. Drain well, then spread out on a baking sheet in a single layer to cool.

Place the grains in a medium mixing bowl and add the peanuts, radishes, carrots, greens, lemon juice and oil. Stir well to combine, then taste for seasoning and adjust to your liking with salt and pepper. Toss with chopped herbs, divide between two bowls and serve.

Peanut-Field Pea Salad with Lemon Ricotta

Although peanuts are botanically a legume, they're more closely related to field peas than nuts, so it makes sense to me to combine field peas and peanuts in one bite with some creamy ricotta and the sweetness and tang of tomatoes and peppers. If you prefer not to make your own ricotta, simply substitute your favorite good-quality brand. If you don't have access to field peas, other cooked shelling beans will work perfectly fine. We serve this salad at my restaurant, Miller Union, every summer, and it has a hard-core cult following.

For the vinaigrette:

1 garlic clove

½ teaspoon kosher salt

2 tablespoons sherry vinegar

½ teaspoon Dijon mustard

Freshly ground black pepper

¼ cup extra-virgin olive oil

For the lemon ricotta:

Zest of 2 lemons

¼ cup lemon juice

2 teaspoons fine sea salt

3 cups whole milk

1 cup heavy cream

For the salad:

2 cups field peas, blanched in salted water and shocked in ice water

1 cup shelled boiled peanuts (page 12)

1 large ripe tomato, diced

1 sweet bell pepper, diced

Kosher salt

½ cup dry-roasted peanuts (page 13), lightly crushed

¼ cup chopped mint

serves
-4-

Make the vinaigrette: On a cutting board, finely chop the garlic, then add the salt. Using the side of your knife, rub the garlic and salt against the cutting board until they form a paste. In a small bowl, whisk together the garlic paste, vinegar, mustard and a few cranks of pepper. While whisking, slowly drizzle in the oil until emulsified. *Makes ⅔ cup.*

Make the ricotta: In a small bowl, combine the lemon zest and juice and let sit for 5 minutes. Using a fine-mesh sieve, strain the zest from the juice and discard the zest. Add the salt to the lemon juice and stir until dissolved. In a small saucepot, combine the milk and cream, then add the lemon mixture. DO NOT STIR. Place the pot over medium-low heat just until it starts to simmer, then remove the pan from the heat. Set aside until the mixture reaches room temperature, around 1 hour— by then the mixture will have separated into thick curds and liquid (whey). *Makes 2 cups.*

Using a ladle, gently transfer the milk mixture into a cheesecloth-lined sieve placed over a container, being careful not to break up the curds too much. Let drain for 1 hour, then check the consistency. If the cheese drains for too long and becomes thick, simply add some of the whey from the container back to the cheese and stir well to combine to the desired consistency. Once you've achieved the consistency you like, transfer the cheese to a lidded container and store in the refrigerator until ready to use. The whey can be saved for other uses (store in the refrigerator), such as the Creamy Eggplant & Peanut Toasts on page 18.

Make the salad: In a small bowl, combine the field peas and boiled peanuts. Add the tomato and peppers and toss with 2 tablespoons of vinaigrette (store the remaining vinaigrette in an airtight container in the refrigerator, where it will keep for up to 2 weeks). Season lightly with salt and set aside.

In four shallow bowls, spread 2 to 3 tablespoons of ricotta across the center of each bowl. Evenly divide the salad among the bowls, piling it on top of the ricotta. Top each salad with some of the dry-roasted peanuts and chopped mint, dividing them among the bowls. Serve immediately.

Creamy Eggplant & Peanut Toasts

When eggplant is cooked until it's very soft and tender, there is a delicious nuttiness to it that goes so perfectly with peanuts. This warm spread riffs on the Middle Eastern dish of baba ghanouj, swapping rich peanut butter in the place of tahini and topping it all off with crunchy dry-roasted peanuts for added texture and double peanut flavor.

1 medium eggplant

1 tablespoon bacon fat or extra-virgin olive oil

1 yellow onion, diced

1 garlic clove, minced

2 teaspoons kosher salt, divided

1 teaspoon oregano leaves, finely chopped

½ teaspoon ground cumin

½ teaspoon red pepper flakes

½ teaspoon thyme leaves

¼ cup natural peanut butter (page 14, or store-bought)

¼ cup buttermilk or plain yogurt (or whey from making the ricotta on page 17)

½ cup chopped dry-roasted peanuts (page 13)

2 teaspoons Italian parsley, roughly chopped

Thinly sliced baguette, toasted and brushed with butter, for serving

serves 6 to 8

Preheat the oven to 400° and place a rack in the center position. Using the tip of a paring knife, prick the skin of the eggplant in several places. Put the eggplant in a shallow baking dish and bake until the skin is crisp and dark and the eggplant is very soft inside, about 40 minutes. (Alternatively, you can cook the eggplant on the hottest part of a grill and char it on all sides until creamy in the middle; this will lend it a slightly smoky flavor.) Remove the dish from the oven and let the eggplant cool slightly; leave the oven on.

In a medium skillet, warm the bacon fat or oil over medium-high heat. Add the onion, garlic and 1 teaspoon of salt. Turn the heat down to medium low and cook until the onion is translucent, stirring often. Meanwhile, peel the eggplant, discarding the skin and saving the flesh and juices inside. Add the warm, soft eggplant, plus any of its juices, to the skillet and stir well to combine. Mash the eggplant a little in the pan to break it up, then add the remaining teaspoon of salt and the oregano, cumin, red pepper flakes, thyme and peanut butter and stir well. Add the buttermilk or yogurt, then stir well to combine. Taste for seasoning and adjust to your liking. A little texture in this mixture is fine, but if it seems lumpy, transfer to a food processor and puree until smooth.

Transfer the warm eggplant mixture to a shallow 8-by-8-inch baking dish. Scatter the chopped peanuts over the surface of the dip, transfer to the oven and bake for 10 minutes until hot and bubbly. Remove the eggplant from the oven and let cool slightly. Scatter the parsley over the surface of the dish and serve hot in the baking dish with buttered baguette toasts on the side.

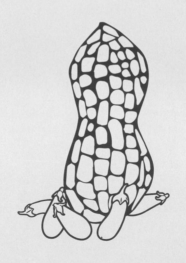

Grilled Okra with Spiced Yogurt & Peanuts

Grilled okra and roasted peanuts with a bath of some creamy-zesty-tangy yogurt may sound like an unusual combination, but these flavors and textures together might just blow your mind. The "two-skewer method" of threading okra pods together across the tops and tips of the pods creates a broad plank, making them easy to turn over a hot grill without worrying about individual pods falling through the grates.

1 cup whole-milk Greek yogurt	1 teaspoon kosher salt, divided
1 large garlic clove	1 pound fresh okra pods
1 lemon	2 to 3 tablespoons peanut oil
1 teaspoon ground cumin	½ cup chopped dry-roasted peanuts (page 13)
1 teaspoon ground coriander	
1 teaspoon red pepper flakes	3 to 4 tablespoons chopped mint

serves 4 to 6

Submerge several six-inch wooden skewers in water to soak.

Preheat a grill. If using a charcoal grill, place natural charcoal and/or wood and light. Let the flames flare up and die down before cooking on them. If using a gas grill, heat to medium high. Prepare the remaining ingredients while the grill warms up.

Place the yogurt in a medium mixing bowl. Using a rasp grater, finely grate the garlic and lemon zest over the yogurt. Cut the zested whole lemon in half and squeeze the juice over a small fine-mesh sieve into the yogurt. Add the cumin, coriander, red pepper flakes and ½ teaspoon of salt. Stir well to combine, then cover and refrigerate until ready to use.

Arrange the okra pods on a work surface with all the tips facing in the same direction. Holding the pods in place with one hand, use your other hand to thread a skewer about ½ inch from the top of each pod, just below the cap of the okra. Thread a second skewer about ½ inch from the bottom of each pod, just above the tapered tip, creating a row of secured pods that resembles a plank of okra. Be sure to leave the ends of the skewer exposed about an inch to prevent the pods from falling off. Repeat with more skewers and okra until all the pods are secured and planked. Brush both sides of the okra planks with oil; sprinkle both sides evenly with the remaining ½ teaspoon of salt.

Place the okra planks on the hot grill. Cook until the pods begin to char slightly, about 2 minutes, then flip and grill the opposite side for about 2 minutes longer. Transfer the grilled okra to a platter; when cool enough to handle, remove the skewers.

To serve as a vegetable side: Layer the yogurt, okra, peanuts and fresh mint onto a plate or platter. To serve as an appetizer: Place the yogurt in a serving bowl and top with peanuts and fresh mint. Place the grilled okra pods around the bowl and serve warm or at room temperature, encouraging your guests to eat with their hands.

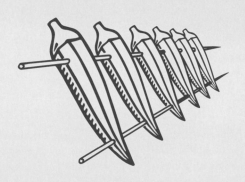

Roasted Delicata Squash with Peanut-Sesame-Squash-Seed Dukkah

Dukkah is an Egyptian recipe that functions as both spice blend and condiment. The ingredients are subject to interpretation (many Egyptian households pride themselves on their own family blend), but the basic formula features chopped hazelnuts or pistachios mixed with sesame seeds and spices. I created my own version of dukkah to top cubes of sweet roasted delicata squash, and, in an attempt to remain authentic to my region, I put Georgia peanuts at the forefront. The result is completely addictive and goes way beyond a squash topping. Roasting the squash in green peanut oil brings out its natural earthy flavor and connects it to the crunchy dukkah that will cover it. Bonus: Unlike most fall squash, delicata has a thin, tasty skin, so there's no need to peel it (a relief, given its deep ridges and crevices).

---

2 medium or 3 small delicata squash (about 2½ pounds total)

2 teaspoons kosher salt, divided

6 tablespoons green peanut oil, divided (I like to use oil from Oliver Farms)

½ cup sesame seeds, toasted (I like to use benne seeds from Anson Mills)

½ cup dry-roasted peanuts (page 13)

1 tablespoon ground coriander

1 tablespoon ground cumin

1 tablespoon freshly ground black pepper

serves 4 to 6

Preheat the oven to 350° and arrange racks in the upper and lower thirds of the oven. Place the squash in a large bowl and rinse well, then rub vigorously with a kitchen towel to remove any traces of dirt in the crevices. Transfer the squash to a cutting board and cut each in half crosswise. Place each half cut side down and carefully slice in half lengthwise. Using a spoon, scrape the seeds and surrounding flesh into a medium bowl and set aside.

Cut the squash quarters into ½-inch cubes (leave the skin on). In a large bowl, toss the squash cubes with 1 teaspoon of salt and 4 tablespoons of oil. Add the remaining 2 tablespoons of oil to the bowl with the squash flesh and seeds and toss to coat.

Line two baking sheets with parchment paper or silicone mats. Arrange the squash cubes in a single layer on one of the sheets; on the other sheet, arrange the squash seeds and press firmly into a single layer, making sure to smoosh the pockets of squash flesh down into as flat a layer as possible. Place the cubed squash on the lower rack of the oven, and the seeds on the upper rack. Bake for 25 to 30 minutes or until the squash is tender and the seeds are lightly browned and the surrounding flesh is dried. (Depending on your oven, this could take more or less time, so start checking frequently after 20 minutes.) Remove both pans from the oven and let cool.

Make the dukkah: In a food processor, combine the roasted squash seeds and the flesh that surrounded them, sesame seeds, peanuts, coriander, cumin, black pepper and the remaining teaspoon of salt. Process until the mixture resembles the texture of coarse cornmeal. Transfer the dukkah to a small bowl and reserve. Before serving, reheat the squash in the oven until it is hot all the way through, 7 to 10 minutes. Toss the hot squash with 4 to 6 tablespoons of the dukkah and serve. Save the remaining squash-seed-spice blend for sprinkling on greens, meat, fish or bread; the dukkah will keep in an airtight container in a cool, dry spot for up to 4 weeks.

Braised Greens & Peanuts with Hot Sauce

Throwing some peanuts in a pot of Southern-style braised greens may not seem like a revelation, but I absolutely fell in love with this simple tweak on a classic dish. The peanuts simmer for some time in the cooking liquid—or pot likker, as we call it in the South—but they don't lose their crunch, which provides a welcome contrast to the silky, tender greens. Also, the hot sauce is key, so be sure to have some at the ready.

1½ pounds greens, such as collards, kale, turnip tops or any combination

2 ounces slab bacon, cut into cubes

1 yellow onion, diced

4 garlic cloves, thinly sliced

4 teaspoons kosher salt

½ teaspoon freshly ground black pepper

1 cup dry-roasted peanuts (page 13)

Your favorite hot sauce

If the stems of the greens are thick, remove them, then roughly chop the greens. The stems can be incorporated too, if they're not too woody; thinly slice them and set aside.

Place the bacon in a large 8- to 10-quart pot set over medium-low heat. Stir frequently until some of the fat has rendered into the bottom of the pot. Add the onion, garlic, greens stems (if using), salt and pepper and turn the heat up to medium high. Stir frequently and cook until the onion begins to turn translucent, about 5 minutes. Add the chopped greens and just enough water to cover them, about 3 quarts. Add the peanuts and simmer until the greens are very tender, about 30 minutes or more. Taste the greens and the cooking liquid, and adjust the seasoning as needed. Transfer the greens and all the pot likker to a large bowl and serve them with a healthy dose of your favorite hot sauce.

Chicken & Cabbage Salad with Peanuts & Mango

This salad is spicy, crunchy, zesty, tangy and delicious. The idea is inspired by those "Chinese" chicken salads of the 1970s. I took some global cues, with accents from Vietnam and Thailand as well. It's a melting-pot salad for sure, but the main takeaway is the ground peanuts, which infiltrate every bite with a nutty, sweet crunch that satisfies.

For the nuoc cham:

¼ cup fresh lime juice (from about 3 limes)

2 tablespoons fish sauce

2 tablespoons plus 2 teaspoons sugar

1 garlic clove, finely grated on a rasp grater

1 small hot chile pepper, minced

serves
·4·

For the salad:

1 large head Napa cabbage, sliced into ¼-inch strips, washed and dried

1 ripe mango, peeled and diced

¼ cup mint leaves, chopped

1 bunch scallions, thinly sliced

1 small hot chile pepper, minced

2 tablespoons tamari

2 grilled or roasted chicken breasts, thinly sliced

1 cup crispy chow mein noodles

1¼ cups dry-roasted peanuts (page 13), ground for 1 minute in a food processor

Make the *nuoc cham*: In a mixing bowl, whisk the lime juice, fish sauce, sugar, garlic and chile pepper vigorously until the sugar completely dissolves. *Makes ½ cup.*

Make the salad: In a large bowl, combine the cabbage, mango, mint, scallions and chile pepper. Add the tamari and *nuoc cham* and toss. Add the chicken, noodles and peanuts and toss to combine. Serve immediately.

Crispy Chicken Thighs with Spicy Peanut Sauce

Fried chicken thighs with a succulent, moist interior only get better with this boss peanut sauce. I love the tangy zing that it adds to the crispy-skinned chicken, but don't stop there. You can (and should) use the sauce on noodles, vegetables, roasted meats or fish. If you can't find boneless skin-on chicken thighs, then purchase bone-in pieces and remove the bones yourself (insert the tip of a sharp knife along the length of the bone along the flesh side to expose it, then remove the bone). This shallow-fry naked chicken gets extra-crispy skin that crackles under the gooey peanut sauce.

For the spicy peanut sauce:

½ cup natural peanut butter (page 14, or store-bought)

1 garlic clove, finely grated on a rasp grater

½-inch knob fresh ginger, peeled and finely grated on a rasp grater (about 1 tablespoon)

Juice of 1 lime

2 tablespoons soy sauce or tamari

3 tablespoons Vietnamese chile-garlic sauce

For the crispy chicken thighs:

1 cup peanut oil

4 boneless, skin-on chicken thighs

Kosher salt and freshly ground black pepper

3 scallions, thinly sliced, for garnish

serves · 4 ·

Make the sauce: In a medium bowl, combine the peanut butter, garlic, ginger, lime juice, soy sauce and chile-garlic sauce. Stir until well combined and set aside until ready to serve. Depending on the style of peanut butter you use, the sauce varies in viscosity. If the sauce is too thick, simply stir in some water by the tablespoon until it reaches a pourable consistency. *Makes 1 cup.*

Cook the chicken thighs: In a medium skillet set over medium heat, heat the oil until it registers 325° on a deep-fry thermometer. Season the chicken on both sides with salt and pepper. Carefully place the chicken thighs, skin side down, in the pan. Cook for 10 minutes undisturbed, until the skin is golden and crisp, then carefully turn over and cook on the other side for 5 to 7 minutes longer. If the oil begins to smoke, decrease the heat. Carefully transfer the chicken to a paper towel–lined plate.

Let the chicken rest for 5 to 7 minutes, then slice into thick strips and transfer to a serving plate or platter. Spoon some of the peanut sauce over the top and garnish with scallions. Serve immediately.

(Save any remaining peanut sauce and serve with the Summer Squash Noodles on page 30.)

Peanut-Crusted Flounder with Sweet Onion, Brown Butter & Lemon

I grew up in coastal South Georgia, where flounder is a standard boat catch and a staple on the menus of the many seafood shacks in the area. It's a delicate white fish that becomes very unpleasant and pasty if it's overcooked, so err on the side of just barely cooking it through. The peanut crust will give you all the texture you want as contrast.

½ cup (1 stick) unsalted butter

1 medium yellow onion, halved and thinly sliced

Kosher salt and freshly ground black pepper

2 lemons, divided

1½ pounds flounder fillet, or other mild white fish

1¼ cups dry-roasted peanuts (page 13), ground for 1 minute in a food processor

8 ounces baby spinach

4 tablespoons chopped parsley

serves **4** *to* **6**

Preheat the oven to 350° and place a rack in the center position.

In a saucepan, melt the butter over medium-low heat and continue to cook until it foams and subsides and begins to turn golden brown, 15 to 20 minutes. Remove the pan from the heat and set aside.

On a rimmed baking sheet, arrange the onion slices in a single layer and season generously with salt and pepper. Drizzle with 2 tablespoons of the browned butter and toss to combine. Return the onions to a single layer and bake for 15 minutes. Turn on the broiler element of your oven, and finish cooking the onions under high heat until they're tender and lightly browned, about 2 minutes. Let cool. Return the oven to 350°.

Slice one lemon paper-thin and remove the seeds. Cut the slices into quarters and reserve.

If the flounder is thin, trim the ends at the tail side, so that each fillet is of an even thickness (this will keep them from overcooking). Remove any pin bones.

Prepare a small baking sheet by coating it with 1 tablespoon of the reserved brown butter. Arrange the flounder on the baking sheet so the fillets are touching. Season the fillets with salt and pepper.

In a small bowl, combine the ground peanuts with 2 tablespoons of the reserved brown butter. Press the peanut mixture evenly onto the surface of the fillets. Scatter the lemon slices around the edges of the pan and drizzle them with 1 tablespoon of the brown butter. Bake the flounder for 10 minutes, or until the fish is slightly opaque at the edges.

While the fish is cooking, in a medium skillet over medium heat, add the spinach and 1 tablespoon of the brown butter. Cook, stirring occasionally, until the spinach has completely wilted and cooked down, about 3 minutes. Season with salt and pepper. Add the broiled onions to the spinach, toss to combine and keep warm while you finish the fish.

After the flounder has cooked for 10 minutes, turn the oven to broil. Broil the fish for 5 to 6 minutes, watching closely, until the peanuts are lightly browned and the fish is just finished cooking through but is not well done. Watch the peanuts closely as well, and remove them from the broiler immediately if they start to get dark. If the fish needs more time to cook but the peanuts might risk burning, turn the broiler off and bake at 350° until the fish reaches the desired doneness. Remove the fish from the oven and, using the back of a spoon or a spatula, gently smooth the peanut mixture back down across the fish. (The fish fillets will shrink a bit and give off some liquid during cooking, so this helps redistribute the crust if it shifted. Also, if there are any browned bits of nuts, the majority of them should stick to the back of the spoon or spatula.)

In a small saucepan, reheat the remaining 1 tablespoon of brown butter and add the juice of the remaining lemon. Season lightly with salt, and simmer until the salt dissolves. Divide the spinach among 4 dinner plates. Lay the fish on top of the spinach and spoon some of the brown butter–lemon sauce over the top. Garnish with the roasted lemon slices and parsley and serve immediately.

Summer Squash "Noodles" with Spicy Peanut Sauce

This recipe requires a spriralizer, a kitchen device that turns fruits or vegetables into noodle strands by carving them into spirals, like a corkscrew cutter. It also happens to be quick, easy and ridiculously healthy. I was hesitant to join the recent spiralizer craze, but I have to admit that it's a really fun tool that changes the way you perceive vegetables. And remember that crazy delicious peanut sauce from the crispy chicken thighs on page 26? It's back!

2 pounds mixed summer squash

2 tablespoons peanut oil

½ pound green beans, ends trimmed, sliced crosswise into ¼-inch pieces

Salt and freshly ground pepper

1 teaspoon fresh lemon juice

½ cup Spicy Peanut Sauce (page 26), or more to taste

⅔ cup dry-roasted peanuts (page 13), ground for 1 minute in a food processor

¼ cup chopped basil

Trim the ends off the squash and use a spiralizer to cut the squash into thin noodles.

In a wide skillet, warm the oil over medium heat. Add the squash noodles and green beans to the pan and season with salt and pepper. Cook for 4 to 5 minutes, stirring frequently, until the vegetables are tender but still crisp. Add the lemon juice, peanut sauce and peanuts and stir well to combine. Garnish with basil and serve immediately.

Nam Sod Pork
with Peanuts & Cabbage

If you've never tried making *nam sod*, a Thai ground pork and peanut appetizer served with raw cabbage, you'll be surprised at just how easy it is. I've eaten it for years at my favorite Thai restaurant here in Atlanta, but never attempted to make it myself until now. The peanuts are such an important part of this authentic dish; it wouldn't be the same without them. Beverage tip: It's a surprisingly great appetizer to accompany Champagne.

2 teaspoons peanut oil

1 tablespoon minced hot chile pepper

2 tablespoons minced fresh ginger

1 tablespoon minced garlic

1 shallot, very thinly sliced

1½ pounds ground pork

4 limes (2 juiced, 2 sliced into wedges for garnish), divided

1 teaspoon red pepper flakes

3 tablespoons fish sauce

1 cup dry-roasted peanuts (page 13), ground for 1 minute in a food processor

1 head cabbage, separated into individual leaves and washed

1 small cucumber, halved lengthwise and thinly sliced

1 bunch mint leaves, chopped

1 bunch cilantro leaves, chopped

serves
·4·

In a wide skillet, warm the oil over medium heat. Add the chile, ginger, garlic and shallot and cook for 1 minute. Add the pork and cook for 7 to 8 minutes, stirring frequently, until the pork is no longer pink. Add the juice of 2 limes, the red pepper flakes and the fish sauce and cook for 1 to 2 minutes longer. Taste for seasoning when the pork is completely cooked through and adjust as needed. Add the ground peanuts to the pork and stir well to incorporate.

Remove the skillet from the heat and spoon the hot pork mixture into the cabbage leaves. Top with the cucumber slices, mint and cilantro and serve with lime wedges.

Snapper in Peanut-Tomato Broth with Coconut Rice

I tested this Indonesian-inspired stew on my family while we were vacationing at the beach, and I warned them: "I have a deadline and we need to eat this tonight." Although I was met with some skepticism at first, they loved the dish, and this recipe became an instant hit. It really is one of my favorites in this volume. The tender pieces of snapper are lightly poached and enveloped in the peanut-butter-tomato-lime broth, and the bok choy adds a juicy crunch and boosts the vegetable factor.

For the rice:

1 cup jasmine or basmati rice

1 tablespoon minced lemongrass

1 tablespoon minced garlic

1 teaspoon fine sea salt

One 14-ounce can coconut milk

For the stew:

1 tablespoon vegetable oil

1 yellow onion, diced

1 red bell pepper, diced

2 garlic cloves, minced

1 tablespoon kosher salt

2 cups peeled and diced tomatoes, or one 14-ounce can diced tomatoes

½ cup natural peanut butter (page 14, or store-bought)

½ teaspoon turmeric

2 teaspoons paprika

Juice of 1 lime

1½ pounds snapper fillet with skin, pinbones removed, cut into 1-inch cubes

Freshly ground black pepper

2 heads baby bok choy, cut into bite-size pieces

Cilantro leaves, for garnish

serves ·4·

Make the rice: In a small saucepan over medium heat, combine the rice, lemongrass, garlic, salt, ½ cup of water and the coconut milk. Bring to a boil, then reduce the heat to low and cover. Cook for 15 to 20 minutes or until the rice is tender and the liquid has been absorbed. Remove the pan from the heat and set aside.

Make the stew: In a medium high-sided sauté pan, warm the oil over medium heat. Add the onion, pepper, garlic and salt and stir to combine. Cook for 5 minutes, stirring frequently, until the onion is translucent. Add the tomatoes, peanut butter, turmeric and paprika and stir well to incorporate. Bring the mixture to a simmer, stir in the lime juice and ½ cup of water, and remove the pan from the heat. Working in batches, transfer the mixture to a blender and blend until smooth (make sure to leave a vent for steam to escape).

Season the snapper liberally with salt and pepper. Return the tomato-peanut puree to the sauté pan and set over medium heat. Add the bok choy and simmer until tender, about 4 minutes. Add the seasoned snapper and gently stir until the fish is well coated. Reduce the heat to medium low, then cover and simmer for 5 minutes or just until the fish is cooked through but still tender. Taste for seasoning and adjust as needed.

Using a large scoop, divide the cooked rice to form four firm balls, and place a rice ball in the center of four wide soup bowls. Spoon the fish stew over the rice. Garnish with cilantro and serve immediately.

Peanut Pasta with Broccoli & Peanut Breadcrumbs

When I make pasta dough, I like to experiment with alternative flours, and this one was a real triumph. The peanut flour adds protein structure to the dough and the flavor has a peanut-y sweetness to it. I think it's a perfect pairing with the sweet onions and broccoli.

¼ cup shelled dry-roasted peanuts (page 13)

2 tablespoons chopped parsley

¼ cup dry breadcrumbs

1 cup 00 pasta flour (or unbleached all-purpose flour), plus extra for rolling

1 cup peanut flour

1 cup egg yolks (approximately 14 eggs, depending on the size of the yolks)

¼ cup kosher salt for pasta water, plus more for seasoning

4 tablespoons olive oil, divided

1 onion, halved and thinly sliced

2 garlic cloves, sliced

1 teaspoon red pepper flakes, divided

2 small heads or 1 large head broccoli, cut into florets and stems cut into bite size pieces

1 teaspoon flaky sea salt

½ lemon

In a food processor, coarsely chop the peanuts. Add the parsley and breadcrumbs and pulse until just combined. Set aside.

In a medium bowl, combine the pasta and peanut flours. Make a small well in the center of the flours and place the yolks in the well. With a fork or your fingers, stir the yolks in a circular pattern, gradually pulling flour from the edges into the well, until a dough forms. When the mixture gets too thick to stir, turn the contents of the bowl out onto a clean surface dusted with pasta flour, and knead until fully combined and uniform, about 1 minute. Form the pasta dough into a ball, flatten into a 1-inch-thick disk and dust with pasta flour. Wrap tightly in plastic wrap and set aside at room temperature for at least 30 minutes or up to 1 hour.

Place a 6-quart pot over medium heat and fill with 1 gallon of water and ¼ cup of kosher salt.

When you're ready to roll out the dough, dust a flat surface with flour and, using a rolling pin, roll the dough out to ½ inch thickness. Using a pasta roller, and working in batches, run small amounts of the dough through the machine on the widest setting first. Fold the dough into thirds and run through the machine again. Repeat this step one more time; the dough should be uniformly shaped and the same width as the roller. Continue to pass the dough through, adjusting the setting on the machine to make the dough thinner each time. As you're working, you can cut the dough into pieces so it's easier to manage and pass through. Roll each sheet of dough out to about the thickness of $\frac{1}{16}$ inch. Trim the sheets of dough into 10- to 12-inch-long pieces. Then, using a fettuccine cutter attachment, run the dough through one last time to cut into uniform noodles. (If you don't have the attachment, cut your noodles by hand with a knife or a pinwheel cutter.) Lay the noodles out on a floured surface and let them rest while you finish the dish.

Turn the salted water on the stove to high heat. In a wide skillet over medium heat, warm 2 tablespoons of oil. Add the onion and season with kosher salt. Cook for 5 to 6 minutes, until slightly browned, then add the garlic and ½ teaspoon of red pepper flakes and cook for 1 minute longer. Add the broccoli florets and stems and the remaining 2 tablespoons of oil. Reduce the heat to medium and cook for 1 minute longer, then turn off the heat until you're ready to add the noodles.

Meanwhile, add the noodles to the boiling water and stir immediately to keep them from sticking to each other. Cook the noodles for 2 to 3 minutes, then drain well, reserving 1 cup of the pasta water. Add the pasta to the skillet with the broccoli, along with about 2 tablespoons of the reserved pasta water.

Stir the contents of the pan well, until the ingredients are combined and the pasta water has reduced to a thin sauce that coats the noodles. Remove from the heat, sprinkle with sea salt and squeeze lemon juice over the pasta in the pan; toss to combine. Transfer the pasta to a serving bowl or individual plates and top with some of the breadcrumb-peanut mixture. Garnish with the remaining ½ teaspoon of red pepper flakes and serve immediately.

Peanut & Strawberry Parfaits

I love a parfait. It's so old-fashioned, yet it wows every time. This take on a classic PB&J combination of roasted peanuts and juicy strawberries bathed in a supple buttermilk custard will have you marking this page and revisiting it often.

For the buttermilk custard:

1 cup whole milk

2 tablespoons cornstarch

¼ cup sugar

⅛ teaspoon kosher salt

1 large egg

¼ teaspoon pure vanilla extract

2 tablespoons unsalted butter

1 cup buttermilk

For the parfaits:

1 cup hulled and sliced strawberries, plus more for garnish

½ cup finely chopped dry-roasted peanuts (page 13)

¼ cup Salted Peanut Toffee (page 38), finely chopped in food processor, plus more for garnish

makes
•4•

Make the buttermilk custard: In a medium heavy-bottomed saucepan, warm the whole milk over medium heat. Meanwhile, in a medium bowl, whisk together the cornstarch, sugar and salt. Add the egg and whisk until smooth, about 1 minute. When the milk comes to a boil, remove the pan from the heat. While whisking quickly, slowly pour one third of the hot milk into the egg mixture to temper the eggs. Pour the tempered-egg mixture into the pot with the remaining hot milk, and whisk well to combine.

Return the pot to the stove and place over medium-low heat. Cook the mixture until thickened, whisking continuously. When the mixture just begins to bubble, remove it from the heat immediately and stir in the vanilla and butter. Whisk until the butter has melted and is incorporated. Transfer to a medium bowl and cover with plastic wrap, pressing the plastic onto the surface of the custard to prevent a skin from forming. Refrigerate until chilled. Whisk the chilled custard with the buttermilk until smooth, then refrigerate until ready to use. *Makes 2 cups.*

Assemble the parfaits: Place four 8-ounce glasses or bowls on a work surface. Spoon 2 tablespoons of the fresh strawberries into the bottom of each glass. Add 1 tablespoon of peanuts, followed by ¼ cup of the custard and 1 tablespoon of the toffee. Repeat the layers until you reach the top of the vessel. Garnish with strawberries and toffee and serve immediately.

Salted Peanut Toffee

Making homemade toffee is so incredibly easy that you'll wonder why you ever bought it in the first place. This salty-sweet peanut-y version is an addictive snack, but it also makes a great add-in to cookies, coffee cake, ice cream or Chex mix and popcorn. Safety tip: Always use caution when handling hot sugar.

½ cup (1 stick) unsalted butter

¾ cup sugar

2 teaspoons corn syrup

makes **1** *quart*

1 teaspoon fine sea salt

1¼ cups dry-roasted peanuts (page 13), ground for 1 minute in a food processor

Line a baking sheet with a silicone mat or coat with nonstick cooking spray.

In a saucepan over high heat, combine the butter, sugar, corn syrup, salt and 2 tablespoons of water. When the mixture comes to a boil, place a lid on the pot to avoid evaporation, reduce the heat to medium high and cook for 5 minutes. Remove the lid and insert insert a candy thermometer, then continue to cook with the lid off until the mixture registers 310° on the thermometer. (If you don't have a candy thermometer, wait until the mixture turns a medium golden brown color before removing from the heat.) Turn the heat off and, using a large, rigid metal spoon, immediately stir in the peanuts.

Carefully transfer the hot mixture to the prepared baking sheet. Using the back of the metal spoon, spread the mixture into a single layer. Let the toffee cool for at least 30 minutes before attempting to touch it.

When the toffee is completely cool, break it into small pieces and store in an airtight container for up to 2 weeks.

No-Bake Peanut Butter, ChocoLate & Oat Cookies

This is a riff on one of those recipes using basic household pantry ingredients that has circulated all over America. The original recipe calls for cocoa powder, sugar, milk, oats and peanut butter. I'm giving this version an upgrade with real melted chocolate and dry-roasted peanuts added to the mix.

1 cup semisweet chocolate pieces

¾ cup natural creamy peanut butter (page 14, or store-bought)

¼ cup (½ stick) unsalted butter, cut into chunks

1½ cups rolled oats

1 cup dry-roasted peanuts (page 13)

¼ teaspoon fine sea salt

1 teaspoon pure vanilla extract

makes ·36·

In a small saucepan over medium-low heat, combine the chocolate, peanut butter and butter. Cook, stirring continuously, until the mixture has melted (don't let it come to a boil), then add the oats, peanuts, salt and vanilla. Stir until well combined.

Remove the pan from the heat. Line a baking sheet with wax paper, then drop tablespoonfuls of the mixture on the baking sheet. Transfer to the refrigerator and chill until set, then serve, or transfer the cookies to an airtight storage container. Cover and refrigerate for up to 2 weeks.

Peanut & Honey Tart

I've always been a big fan of peanut butter and honey. I can eat both by the spoonful or combine them to make a satisfying and nostalgic sandwich. These classic flavors are presented here nestled inside a buttery crust. You can take the flavor further and garnish each slice of this dessert with some soft whipped cream, a light drizzle of honey and some roasted ground peanuts.

For the crust:

9 tablespoons unsalted butter, at room temperature

¼ cup granulated sugar

½ cup confectioners' sugar

1 large egg

2 cups unbleached all-purpose flour

¼ teaspoon kosher salt

For the filling:

⅔ cup honey

½ cup sugar

1 teaspoon fine sea salt

1 cup (2 sticks) unsalted butter

2 egg yolks

1 large egg

½ teaspoon pure vanilla extract

3 teaspoons all-purpose flour, sifted

½ cup heavy cream

2 cups chopped dry-roasted peanuts (page 13)

Make the crust: In the bowl of a stand mixer fitted with the paddle attachment, cream the butter and sugars by mixing for 2 to 3 minutes, or until well combined and light yellow in color. Stop to scrape down the side of the bowl with a rubber spatula as needed. Add the egg and beat until it's been fully incorporated. Combine the flour and salt together, then add to the mixer in thirds, mixing until just combined after each addition. Wrap the dough in plastic and refrigerate for at least 2 to 3 hours. The dough can be made ahead up to 2 days in advance.

Preheat the oven to 325° and place a rack in the center position. On a lightly floured surface, roll the dough out into a circle about ⅛ inch thick and 11 inches in diameter. Transfer the dough to a 10-inch fluted tart pan with a removable bottom and, using the tips of your fingers, press the dough into the sides so that it is molded to the shape of the pan. Prick the crust with the tines of a fork and refrigerate for 10 minutes. Bake the crust for 10 to 15 minutes, or until light golden in color (it will continue to cook when the filling is added, so don't worry if it's not completely baked). Remove from the oven and let cool.

Make the filling: Keep the oven at 325°. In a medium saucepan over high heat, combine the honey, sugar, salt and butter and bring to a boil. Remove from the heat and let the mixture sit in the pan for 15 minutes to cool a bit. Meanwhile, in a medium bowl, whisk the egg yolks, whole egg and vanilla together and set aside. Return the saucepan to low heat and whisk the flour and cream into the honey mixture. Remove from the heat and, while whisking quickly, gradually pour 1 cup of the hot honey mixture into the egg mixture to temper the eggs. Whisk the egg mixture into the saucepan with the honey mixture until combined. Place a fine-mesh sieve over a medium bowl and pour the finished mixture through it into a bowl.

Place the peanuts in the parbaked tart crust and pour the filling over the nuts. Gently shake the pan to evenly distribute the filling, then transfer to the oven and bake for 15 to 20 minutes until the filling is set. Remove from the oven and let cool on a rack until ready to serve.

Banana Cake
with Peanut Butter Frosting

Pamela Moxley, the pastry chef at my restaurant, Miller Union, came up with this cake, which plays off the classic American combination of peanut butter and banana. Feel free to dress it up with some crushed Salted Peanut Toffee (page 38) scattered across the top if you have any left over. If you want to go way over the top, fill the center with caramelized bananas and crumbled bacon for an all-shook-up Elvis situation.

For the cake:

5 tablespoons unsalted butter, plus extra for greasing

1¾ cups cake flour, plus extra for the pans

3 overripe bananas

2 tablespoons sour cream

2 large eggs

1 teaspoon pure vanilla extract

1 cup sugar

½ cup all-purpose flour

1 teaspoon baking soda

¾ teaspoon baking powder

½ teaspoon fine sea salt

For the peanut butter frosting:

1 cup (2 sticks) unsalted butter, at room temperature

1 cup confectioners' sugar, sifted after measuring

⅛ teaspoon fine sea salt

¼ teaspoon pure vanilla extract

1¾ cups unsweetened natural peanut butter (page 14, or store-bought)

Make the cake: Preheat the oven to 325° and place a rack in the center position. Grease and flour two 8-inch round cake pans.

In a medium mixing bowl, mash the bananas with a fork until smooth. Add the sour cream, eggs, vanilla and sugar. Whisk until the mixture is smooth and the sugar has dissolved, then set aside.

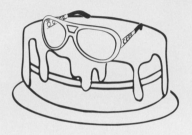

Over a large bowl, sift together the cake flour, all-purpose flour, baking soda, baking powder and salt. Transfer the flour mixture to the bowl of a stand mixer fitted with the paddle attachment. Add the butter to the flour mixture and mix at medium speed until it becomes a crumbly cornmeal-like texture, about 2 minutes. Add half of the banana mixture and mix at medium speed for 1 minute. Add the remaining banana mixture and beat at low speed just until incorporated. Divide the cake batter evenly between the two prepared pans. Carefully place the pans in the oven and bake for 12 to 15 minutes or until a skewer inserted into the center comes out clean. Remove the pans from the oven and place on a rack. Let cool completely in the cake pans.

Make the frosting: In the bowl of a stand mixer fitted with the paddle attachment, mix the butter, sugar, salt and vanilla at medium speed for 2 to 3 minutes, until all the sugar has been absorbed and the mixture becomes fluffy. Add the peanut butter and mix at medium speed until fully incorporated, approximately 2 minutes.

When the cakes are fully cooled, set up to frost them. Place a small dollop of frosting in the center of a cake plate. To turn the first cake layer out of the pan, support the surface with the palm of your hand and carefully lay it top side down on the cake plate. Spoon about a third of the frosting onto the cake layer and spread it evenly across the surface. Remove the second cake layer from the pan and place it top side up on the frosted surface. Spoon the remaining frosting onto the top of the cake and carefully spread it over the top and down the sides until it coats the cake evenly. Serve at room temperature. If you're not serving the cake immediately, refrigerate it. For optimal flavor and temperature, take the cake out of the refrigerator an hour or two before serving it.

Thank You!

I'd like to thank the following people and organizations: Rebecca Harrigan, Tamie Cook, Pamela Moxley, the crew at Miller Union, Clay Oliver, the Hardy Brothers, the National Peanut Board, Kaitlyn Goalen, Nick Fauchald, the Short Stack crew and Dovetail Press.

—*Steven Satterfield*

Share your Short Stack cooking experiences with us
(or just keep in touch) via:

 #shortstackeds

 @shortstackeds

 facebook.com/shortstackeditions

 hello@shortstackeditions.com

Colophon

This edition of Short Stack was printed by Stephen Gould Corp. in Richmond, Virginia on Earthchoice HOTS Orange (interior) and Neenah Oxford White (cover) paper. The main text of the book is set in Futura and Jensen Pro, and the headlines are set in Lobster.

Available now at
ShortStackEditions.com: